CU00692484

Below: an out barn near Bainbridge. Right: Grassington

YORKSHIRE

John Potter

MYRIAD

Left: Wensleydale is the largest of the Dales. This broad sweeping northern valley boasts some of the region's finest scenery.

Below: Hardraw Falls.

Just one mile north-east of Bainbridge on the northern side of Wensleydale, Askrigg is a tiny settlement best known as the setting for the popular television series *All Creatures Great and Small*. Above the village sits Askrigg Common and beyond it the distinctive form of Addlebrough.

Above: set in the heart of Wensleydale, Bainbridge has a wide village green with ancient stocks.

Right: Gayle is sited at the foot of Sleddale. Duerley Beck cascades over a series of limestone steps in the centre of the village before rushing below a packhorse bridge.

Right: dominated by its castle, Middleham is situated just two miles from Leyburn between Coverdale and Wensleydale.

Below: Bolton Castle in the small village of Castle Bolton, five miles west of Leyburn. This massive fortress has loomed over Wensleydale since 1379.

Above: the two western Dales of Dentdale and Ribblesdale straddle the border with Cumbria. They are a mix of lush green valleys and wild, windswept moorland.

Right: the Quaker Friends Meeting House at Brigflatts, half a mile from Sedbergh, was built in 1675.

The pretty village of Dent is actually in Cumbria, four miles south-east of Sedbergh, although it lies within the Yorkshire Dales National Park.

Left: busy Malhamdale is famous for its limestone scenery.

Right: the pretty hamlet of Arncliffe lies at the heart of beautiful Littondale.

Below: the tiny village of Hubberholme, named after a Viking chieftain, is located on the Dales Way four and a half miles from Kettlewell. It is famous for its beautiful church and atmospheric pub.

Left: Appletreewick nestles snugly on a south-facing slope above the river Wharfe.

Above: drystone walls and out barns near Kettlewell are typical of the area.

Right: Linton is a characterful village of stone cottages situated seven miles north of Skipton.

Right: the small town of Pateley Bridge has many interesting nooks and crannies and should not be overlooked when travelling through upper Nidderdale.

Below: the old graveyard in Middlesmoor, at the head of Nidderdale. The village clings to the top of a large hill, its stone cottages and cobbled streets huddled together to form a pretty and interesting hamlet.

Above: the ruined Augustinian priory of Bolton Abbey is situated close to Bolton Bridge, the "gateway" to Wharfedale.

The attractive small town of Masham (above) has a cobbled marketplace surrounded by elegant Georgian houses, stone cottages, shops and tearooms. The spire of St Mary's overlooks the town centre.

Above left: the beautiful abbey at Jervaulx.

Left: the river Ure in the city of Ripon, famous for its historic cathedral.

Above: the beautiful windswept fells and attractive patchwork of fields, drystone walls and barns along the valley bottom at Gunnerside make this part of Swaledale a favourite with visitors.

Left: Harewood House, the home of Earl and Countess Lascelles, was built by the York architect John Carr between 1759 and 1772 on the instructions of Edwin Lascelles whose father had made his fortune in the ribbon trade.

Right: the Alhambra Theatre in Bradford was built in 1914 for the musical impressario Frank Laidler, the "King of Pantomime".

Left: the Victoria Theatre, Halifax. Built in a valley seven miles south-west of Bradford, Halifax is the capital of Calderdale. The town owes its prosperity to the wool trade and its town hall was designed by Sir Charles Barry, the architect of the Houses of Parliament.

Right: the Brontë Parsonage Museum at Haworth. The Parsonage is full of paintings, books and papers that belonged to the Brontës. The rooms have been lovingly restored to convey to visitors what life was like for the parson and his family of writers.

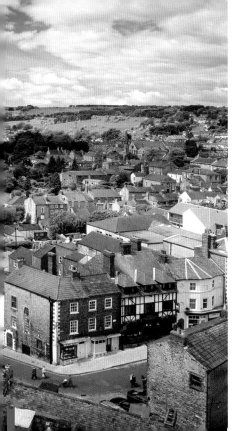

Left: Richmond, the capital of Swaledale, is dominated by its castle keep, part of the massive fortification built by Alan the Red of Brittany, a trusted supporter of William I. Richmond ranks among the most beautiful towns in England, with many elegant Georgian houses, cobbled streets and pretty cottage gardens.

Below: the pretty village of Muker sits proudly above Straw Beck just before it joins the river Swale about one mile east of Thwaite.

Right and below: Leeds, the commercial and financial capital of Yorkshire has many fine buildings. Dominating the heart of the city is Leeds Town Hall, constructed between 1853-58 and designed by Cuthbert Brodrick, the Hull architect. This solid and imposing building is topped by a magnificent domed clocktower rising to 225ft (68m). The owl is a symbol of Leeds that also appears on the city's coat of arms.

Above: the County Arcade presents the visitor with one of the most beautiful shopping environments in the city.

Left: a statue of the former prime minister Harold Wilson graces St George's Square in front of the railway station in Huddersfield. One of the town's most famous sons, the statue was erected in 1999 four years after his death. Located in the West Riding, Huddersfield is an attractive town and boasts 1,660 listed buildings – only Bristol and Westminster have more. The magnificent town hall doubles as a concert hall and is home to the renowned Huddersfield Choral Society.

Left: eight miles west of Halifax, the beautiful town of Hebden Bridge grew rapidly in the 18th and 19th centuries as a result of the wool trade.

Below: Sid's Cafe, one of the locations in Holmfirth used in the long-running television series *Last of the Summer Wine*. This picturesque Pennine town developed rapidly in the 16th century thanks to the cloth industry and its slate and stone mines.

The long, extended valley of Rosedale stretches out in a south-easterly direction from Westerdale Moor and Danby High Moor towards Hartoft End and Cropton Forest.

Above: Mallyan Spout near Goathland, the highest waterfall on the North York Moors. The fall cascades 60ft (18m) down the side of Beck Gorge.

Right: the elegant market town of Pickering is located on the southern edge of the North York Moors.

Right: the tiny and picturesque hamlet of Church Houses nestles between the mighty Rudland Rigg and Blakey Ridge in glorious scenery at the heart of much-loved Farndale.

Below: one of the prettiest country towns in North Yorkshire, Helmsley is a popular destination and an ideal centre for touring the local area.

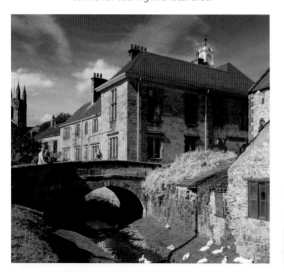

Above: Rievaulx Abbey. This 13th-century church is reputed to have been one of the finest monastic churches in northern Britain and thankfully remains substantially intact. Like all Cistercian houses the location was deliberately secluded from the outside world and this particular site in the depths of the narrow river Rye valley must have provided the monks and lay brethren with a haven of peace and solitude.

Left: Whitby's skyline is dominated by the ruins of St Hilda's Abbey, high up on East Cliff. Just nearby is the parish church of St Mary. Often referred to as Captain Cook's Country, the seaside town of Whitby and the surrounding countryside is where the young James Cook drew his inspiration and learned the seafarer's trade.

Right: Staithes, known locally as "Steers", meaning "landing place", is in a dramatic setting.

Above: Scarborough Castle. Perched on a rocky headland, the ruined castle dominates Scarborough. On a clear day a fantastic view can be enjoyed from the site, which is now in the care of English Heritage. One of the town's main attractions is the Spa Complex with its superb parks, gardens, theatres and conference hall which sits majestically beside the main bathing beach.

Above: the seaside town of Bridlington has two glorious long sandy beaches, miles of elegant promenades and a very pretty and bustling harbour.

Right: opened in 1981, the Humber Bridge links north Lincolnshire and Yorkshire.

Below: the gleaming glass and aluminium marine life centre called The Deep opened in 2002. It stands at the confluence of the rivers Hull and Humber and is part of the vision of reqeneration for the city of Hull.

Below: Spurn Point. Situated on the north bank of the entrance to the river Humber, Spurn Point is a unique place. This three-mile long finger of land snakes out into the Humber estuary and is constantly being reshaped by coastal erosion. Spurn Point is an important location for shipping as it is the home of the Humber lighthouse.

Above: the Shambles, York. One of the highlights of this beautiful city, this meandering medieval street leads up to the Minster. Today it is filled with charming shops; in the Middle Ages it was home to many butchers. Its name comes from the Anglo-Saxon words *shammels* or *fleshshammels* – meaning an open-air slaughterhouse.

The largest Gothic cathedral in northern Europe, York Minster (right) is the seat of the archbishop of York, the second highest office in the Church of England. There has been a church here since 627; work on the current Minster began in 1220 and was not completed until 1472. York Minster is famous for the Great East window, completed in 1408, the largest expanse of medieval stained glass in the world. The view below looks up to the ceiling of the Transept Tower.

Above: Castle Howard. Set amongst magnificent parkland north-east of York, Castle Howard is one of Britain's finest historic houses. It gained fame with television audiences in 1981 when it was used as the setting for *Brideshead Revisited*.

Right: the beautiful town of Knaresborough grew up around the steep sides of the gorge of the river Nidd.

Below: Harrogate. Bettys & Taylors opened their first "continental-style tea room" on Parliament Street, overlooking the colourful Montpellier Gardens, in 1919.

Below: the centre of Sheffield is dominated by the Town Hall which stands at the junction of Surrey Street and Pinstone Street. In front of the Town Hall are the Peace Gardens; the low, curved roof on the far right is that of the Winter Gardens.

Left: Barnsley Town Hall dates from 1933. Sited at the junction of Church Street and Shambles Street at the top of Market Hill, it was erected when Barnsley was still the coal capital of South Yorkshire and it dominates the townscape today.

Right: Stainborough Castle, the recently renovated mock medieval castle built in the grounds of Wentworth Castle, at Stainborough.

Above: Wentworth Woodhouse, whose magnificent East front is the longest frontage of any country house in Europe.

Right: Conisbrough Castle. This magnificent stone castle stands above an important crossing point on the river Don.

Far right: the peaceful ruin of Roche Abbey, nine miles from Doncaster, is in the care of English Heritage.

This fabulous view of the sweeping Robin Hood's Bay was taken from the coastal clifftop path.